A Kid's Book of Experiments With

TIME

SURPRISING Science Experiments

Robert Gardner
and
Joshua Conklin

Enslow Publishing

101 W. 23rd Street
Suite 240
New York, NY 10011
USA

enslow.com

Published in 2016 by Enslow Publishing, LLC
101 W. 23rd Street, Suite 240, New York, NY 10011

Library of Congress Cataloging-in-Publication Data

Gardner, Robert.
A kid's book of experiments with time / by Robert Gardner and Joshua Conklin.
p. cm. — (Surprising science experiments)
Includes bibliographical references and index.
ISBN 978-0-7660-7274-9 (library binding)
ISBN 978-0-7660-7272-5 (pbk.)
ISBN 978-0-7660-7273-2 (6-pack)
1. Time measurements — Experiments — Juvenile literature. 2. Clocks and
watches — Experiments — Juvenile literature. 3. Science — Experiments —
Juvenile literature. 4. Science projects — Juvenile literature. I. Gardner, Robert,
1929-. II. Conklin, Joshua. II. Title.
QB209.5 G3294 2016
529'.7'078—d23

Printed in the United States of America

To Our Readers: We have done our best to make sure all website addresses in this
book were active and appropriate when we went to press. However, the author
and the publisher have no control over and assume no liability for the material
available on those websites or on any websites they may link to. Any comments
or suggestions can be sent by e-mail to customerservice@enslow.com.

Photo Credits: Throughout book: Sapann-Design/Shutterstock.com (colorful
alphabet), Login/Shutterstock.com (series logo), Wiktoria Pawlak/Shutterstock.
com (lightbulb), VLADGRIN/Shutterstock.com (science background), Aleksandrs
Bondars/Shutterstock.com (banners), vector-RGB/Shutterstock.com (arrows);
cover, p. 1 Jeka/Shutterstock.com (girl holding clock); p. 4 Nelson Marques/
Shutterstock.com; p. 7 altanaka/Shutterstock.com; pp. 18, 45 © Robert Gardner;
p. 23 Leyla Ismet/Shutterstock.com; p. 24 Tomruen/Wikimedia Commons/ Lunar_
eclipse_oct_8_2014_Minneapolis_4_46am.png/public domain; p. 27 igordabari/
Shutterstock.com; p. 36 mkos83/Shutterstock.com.

Illustration Credit: Accurate Art, Inc. c/o George Barile.

CONTENTS

Introduction

Time is a constant part of our lives. How many minutes are left in the game? What time will dinner be ready? How long until the school bell rings? These are the types of questions we ask everyday. But have you ever wondered why we measure time in hours and days? Has it ever been measured differently? How did people measure time before they had digital clocks and electronic calendars? Let's take a look at human history and do some experiments to learn more about time.

The Perception of Time

Have you ever been so involved in something that you lost track of time? Or maybe you have been so bored that you stared blankly at a clock. This experiment will take a look at how we perceive time differently when doing various activities.

Experiment 1: Time Test

Things You Will Need:

- timer or clock with alarm
- small weights or old milk jugs filled with water
- book
- good book to read
- partner
- board game
- pen or pencil
- notebook

1. Set a timer or alarm clock to ten minutes.

2. Choose a task to perform during a ten-minute period. Here are some ideas: sit alone in a quiet room, hold up small weights or milk jugs filled with water, read a good book, talk to a friend, or

play a board game. Feel free to also engage in any other activity for the ten minutes. Try not to look at the clock while performing your activity.

3. Record your thoughts after the first session.

4. Set the timer again and do a different activity for ten minutes. Continue with more sessions, recording your thoughts after each one. Which session felt the longest? The shortest? What does your experience tell you about how humans perceive time?

Time Perception: An Explanation

When engaged in enjoyable activities, you probably found that time seemed to move quickly. Perhaps you were surprised when the alarm went off. However, when sitting alone in a room or trying to hold up small weights, time probably seemed to move slowly. Maybe you even thought the timer was broken. You knew the amount of time for each activity was the same but it still *felt* different. Perhaps one reason humans find it important to document time is our inability to accurately tell how fast it is passing.

The Day: A Natural Unit of Time

As we saw in the last experiment, how we experience time can vary. However, some natural units of time, like a day, are fairly easy to measure and perceive. You might believe they have been measured the same way forever. Yet, the way ancient people measured a day varied. Some marked a single day by sunrise to sunrise, others used sunset to sunset, and still others used the time between middays. But what is midday? We can do an experiment to learn more.

Experiment 2:
The Sun's Midday Altitude

Midday occurs when the sun is halfway across the sky. It seldom occurs at noon. You will see why later.

Things You Will Need:

- an adult
- sunny day
- hammer
- stake
- open level ground
- something very straight such as a board
- tape measure, yardstick, or meterstick
- notebook
- pen or pencil
- small stones
- paper
- ruler
- protractor

1. Wait until the sun is close to reaching its zenith (highest point). **Don't look directly at the sun, it can damage your eyes.**

2. Drive a vertical stake into open level ground (ask **an adult** for help if you need it).

3. Watch the stake's shadow. Place a small stone at the end of its shadow about every five minutes.

Do this until you are sure the shadow is growing longer.

4. Using your previously placed stones, find two shadows that had the same length (or nearly so). One should be before midday (before the shortest shadow) and one after.

5. Connect the ends of these two "shadow stones." Use something very straight such as a board, broom handle, or tight string.

6. Mark the middle of the line connecting the ends of these two "shadow stones." It marks the end of the stake's shortest shadow. A line from the stake to the end of the shortest shadow points toward true north. Mark the direction of true north. Save this marking for future experiments.

7. Measure and record the length of the shortest shadow.

8. Measure and record the stake's height. You now have all the information you need to find the sun's midday altitude (angular distance above the horizon).

9. Make a scale drawing of the stake and its shortest shadow. (See Figure 1.)

10. Use a protractor to measure angle a. Angle a was the midday altitude of the sun. What was the sun's midday altitude?

Figure 1

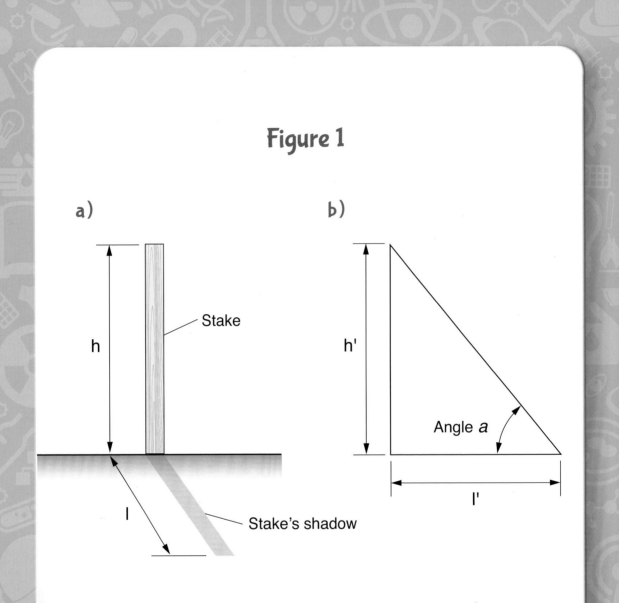

a) The drawing shows a stake and its shortest shadow. The height of the stake is *h*, the length of the shadow is *l*.

b) A scale drawing of the stake and its shadow. The height of the stake is *h'*, the length of its shadow is *l'*, the sun's altitude at midday is angle *a*. You can measure the angle with a protractor.

- Measure the sun's midday altitude at the equinoxes (about March 20 and September 22) and at the solstices (about June 20 and December 21). How do those altitudes compare? How can you explain the similarity and difference?

- Using a clear, plastic hemisphere and a marking pen, map the sun's path across the sky.

- Use a globe and a flashlight to make a model of Earth's seasons.

What Kind of Day Would You Like?

You now know that ancient people marked the passing of a day in different ways. But even today there are three different kinds of days! They are known as a sidereal day, a solar day, and a mean solar day.

The **sidereal day** is preferred by astronomers. During a sidereal day, Earth makes exactly one rotation (360 degrees). Suppose your line of sight runs along a meridian (line of longitude) and points to the sun and also to a distant star beyond the sun (Astronomers can do this even in daylight). One sidereal day is the time it takes for that same star to once again be on that same line of sight. (See Figure 2.)

Figure 2

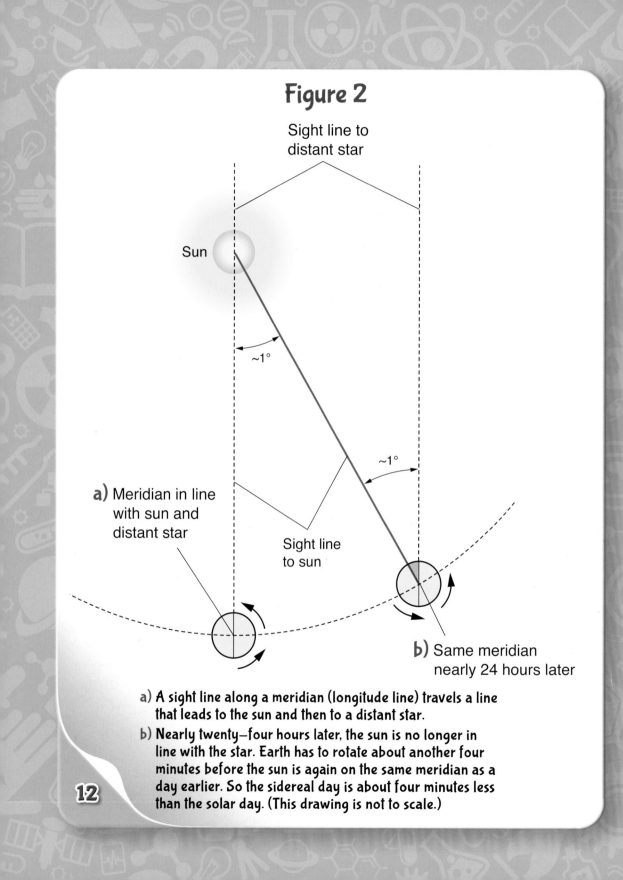

Sight line to distant star

Sun

~1°

~1°

a) Meridian in line with sun and distant star

Sight line to sun

b) Same meridian nearly 24 hours later

a) A sight line along a meridian (longitude line) travels a line that leads to the sun and then to a distant star.

b) Nearly twenty-four hours later, the sun is no longer in line with the star. Earth has to rotate about another four minutes before the sun is again on the same meridian as a day earlier. So the sidereal day is about four minutes less than the solar day. (This drawing is not to scale.)

After one sidereal day, the line of sight along a meridian (line of longitude) is again in line with the distant star. Meanwhile, Earth has moved about one degree along its orbit. That same meridian is no longer on a sight line to the sun. As Figure 2 shows, it will be about four minutes before the line of longitude is again on a sight line to the sun.

The **solar day** is the time between middays. It is the time between successive passings of the sun over the same meridian (line of longitude). After reaching the sidereal day, Earth has to turn another degree to reach midday. Turning one degree takes about four minutes. So the solar day is about four minutes longer than the sidereal day.

Experiment 3: Modeling the Sidereal Day Versus the Solar Day

This experiment will help you understand the difference between a sidereal and solar day.

Things You Will Need:

- distant object such as a tree, pole, or building.
- nearby object that is on a sight line to the distant object

1. Stand so that the near and distant object are on the same line of sight. The distant object represents a star in a galaxy far away. The closer object represents the sun. You represent Earth.

2. Spin around one time. This represents one sidereal day. Everything is still along the same sightline.

3. Move several steps to the right. Your movement represents the additional distance the earth has moved along its orbit in one solar day. While you can still see the distant object, the nearby object is no longer in your direct line of sight. See Figure 3.

The **mean solar day** is the average length of a solar day. Remember, a solar day is the time between successive passages of the sun over a meridian. But not all solar days are equal in length. Experiment 4 will help you understand why.

IDEA for a Science Project

- Show that it takes about four minutes for Earth to turn one degree.

Figure 3

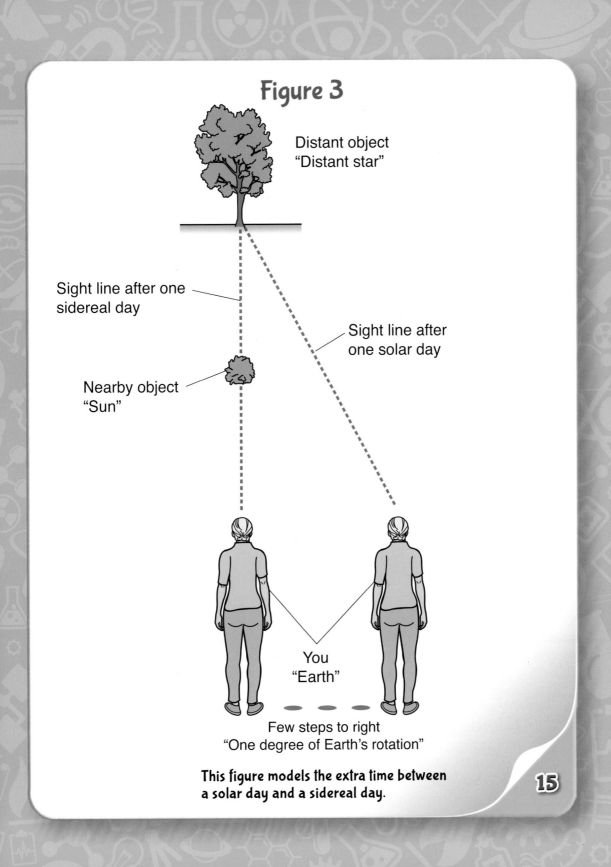

Distant object
"Distant star"

Sight line after one sidereal day

Sight line after one solar day

Nearby object "Sun"

You "Earth"

Few steps to right
"One degree of Earth's rotation"

This figure models the extra time between a solar day and a sidereal day.

Experiment 4: Earth's Speed Along Its Orbit

The Earth orbits the sun once a year. Does the Earth's speed along this orbit remain constant? Let's do an experiment to find out.

Things You Will Need:

- calendar
- globe

1. The fall and spring equinoxes occur around March 20 and September 22. At those times, the sun is above Earth's equator. You can find a representation of the equator on the globe.

   Around December 21, the sun is above the Tropic of Capricorn (the winter solstice). During winter in North America, the sun slowly moves north toward the equator.

   Around June 20, the sun is above the Tropic of Cancer (the summer solstice). It is at its greatest distance north of the equator. It marks the beginning of summer.

2. Count and record the number of winter days between December 21 and March 20. Then count and record the number of summer days between June 20 and September 22.

3. What do these numbers tell you about Earth's speed along its orbit?

The Mean Solar Day

The time between middays (the sun's passage over a local meridian) varies. To take that into account, astronomers invented the mean solar day. The mean solar day is based on an imaginary sun (the mean sun). Unlike the real sun, the mean sun moves at a steady speed along its orbit. It allows us to have uniform time and not have to reset our clocks every day. The mean solar day is exactly twenty-four hours long. However, midday according to clock time and sun time may differ by as much as sixteen minutes. You can find this difference on a globe. It's that elongated figure 8. It is called an analemma (see the photo on page 18). You can more clearly examine an analemma on an actual globe or search for one online. The analemma is a representation of the sun's actual midday point in relation to a clock. At times, the actual midday point is before noon and at times it is after noon.

An analemma shows the difference between sun time and clock time.

Experiment 5: Making an Analemma

You can make an analemma by mapping the sun at exactly the same time every day.

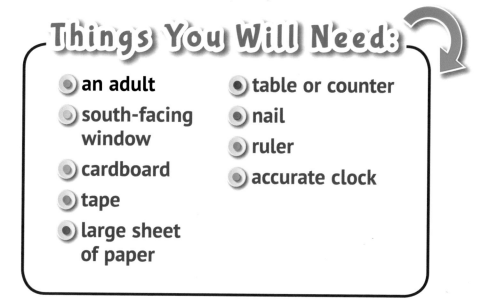

Things You Will Need:

- an adult
- south-facing window
- cardboard
- tape
- large sheet of paper
- table or counter
- nail
- ruler
- accurate clock

1. Have **an adult** help you cover the lower half of a south-facing window with a sheet of cardboard.

2. Place a table or counter near the bottom of the cardboard.

3. Tape a large sheet of paper to the table or counter.

4. Have **an adult** help you use a nail to make a hole through the cardboard. The hole should be about 10 centimeters (4 inches) above the paper on the table. Sunlight coming through the hole will make a bright spot on the paper.

5. At exactly 12 o'clock (noon) mark the bright spot on the paper with a pen or pencil. Try to do this at noon every sunny day. Don't worry if you miss a few days. Even if you mark the spot once a week, you will see a pattern after a few months. Do this faithfully for a year. You will then have an analemma. Is it like the one on a globe?

Why is the spot farther from the window in the winter and closer in the summer? What does the pattern tell you about sun time and clock time?

During what times of the year does the sun move ahead of the clock? At what times is the sun behind the clock?

The Day as a Natural Unit of Time: An Explanation

About Finding Midday: Midday is when the sun is over your meridian (longitude). It is then at its highest point. It will cast its shortest shadow for that day. Your drawing enabled you to measure its midday altitude.

About Orbital Speed: As you found, there are more days of summer (June 21 to September 23) than of winter (December 21 to March 20). The reason is that Earth moves slightly faster along its orbit in our winter than in our summer. Earth is a bit closer to the sun during winter in the northern hemisphere. As a result, the sun's gravity pulls on Earth a little stronger causing Earth to accelerate.

Figure 4 shows that Earth's orbit is not a perfect circle. It is an ellipse. Its slightly elliptical path causes Earth to move faster along its orbit in January and slower in July.

About the analemma: Your analemma revealed that sun time and clock time are different. The noon-hour dot moved left and right as well as farther from and closer to the window. The dot moved farther from the window in winter when the sun was lower in the sky.

The sun was ahead of the clock in the autumn and much of the spring. It was behind the clock during most of the winter and much of the summer.

Figure 4

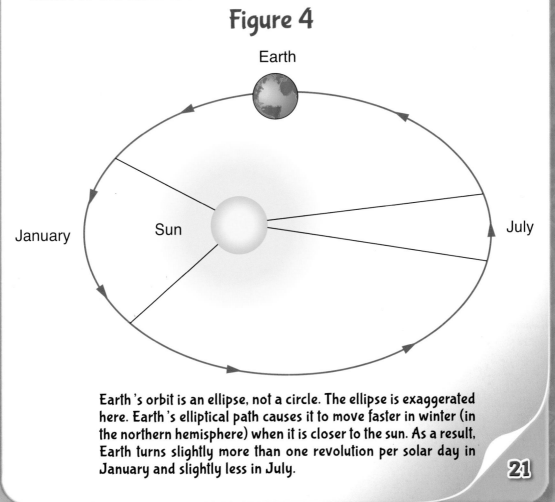

Earth's orbit is an ellipse, not a circle. The ellipse is exaggerated here. Earth's elliptical path causes it to move faster in winter (in the northern hemisphere) when it is closer to the sun. As a result, Earth turns slightly more than one revolution per solar day in January and slightly less in July.

The Lunar Month: A Natural Unit of Time

In the last section we learned about the different kinds of days and how they are measured. The moon's cycle is also used by several religions as a natural unit of time. Their month is the time between full moons or new moons.

Experiment 6: Measuring the Lunar Month

You have probably noticed that the moon's appearance changes. Let's do an experiment to find out more.

Things You Will Need:

- notebook
- pen or pencil
- local paper or Internet access

1. Look for the moon as often as possible. Don't be surprised to see it during the day. Draw what you see in your notebook. Record where and when you see the moon.

2. When you see a full (perfectly circular) moon, record the time and date in your notebook.

3. Continue to look for the moon, drawing and recording the time and the moon's place in the sky.

4. When the moon is again full, record the time and date. How much time has passed since the previous full moon?

5. To find the exact time of full moons, consult your local paper or the Internet.

6. How many lunar months would make one year? What would a calendar based on lunar months look like?

7. Adding the days in twelve lunar months doesn't equal one year (365 days). How could that be managed?

A full moon occurs when Earth is between the moon and the sun.

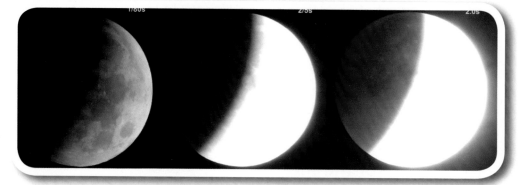

Sometimes a full moon is in Earth's shadow (a lunar eclipse). You can see that Earth's shadow is curved. What causes Earth to have a shadow?

The Lunar Month: An Explanation

The time between one full moon and the next is very nearly 29.5 mean solar days. This means a full moon may sometimes occur during daytime and sometimes at night.

Some cultures alternated 29-day months with 30-day months. However, 12 such months only equal 354 days. The Islamic calendar is 12 lunar months. It doesn't agree with a 365-day year. Other lunar calendars, such as the Chinese and Hindu, add a short month to bring the lunar year into agreement with the solar year.

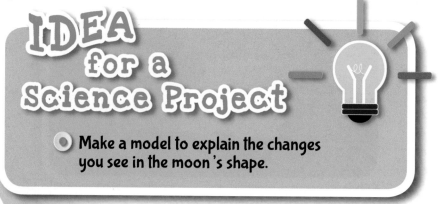

IDEA for a Science Project

● Make a model to explain the changes you see in the moon's shape.

The Year: A Natural Unit of Time

Earth makes one revolution (orbit) around the sun every year. Like the moon's, Earth's orbital time is not equal to a whole number of days. A year is approximately 365.25 days. We manage this extra quarter of a day by having a leap year (a year with an extra day) every four years.

Years, however, have not always been measured by Earth's orbit around the sun. Ancient Egyptians used a star named Sirius to measure the year. A tunnel in a pyramid was directed toward the point where Sirius rose above the horizon. A new year began on the morning Sirius rose with the sun and could be seen from the tunnel.

Their calendar had twelve 30-day months. They just waited five or six days after the calendar year before a new year began.

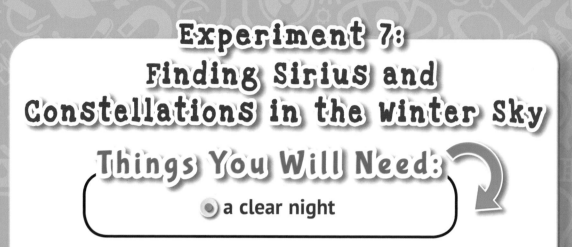

Experiment 7:
Finding Sirius and
Constellations in the Winter Sky

Things You Will Need:
⦿ a clear night

1. Figure 5 is a drawing of the southern sky in the northern hemisphere on a winter evening. Both Orion (the Hunter) and Canis Major (Big Dog) shine brightly in the cold winter sky. Sirius is part of Canis Major and is the brightest star in the sky.

Figure 5

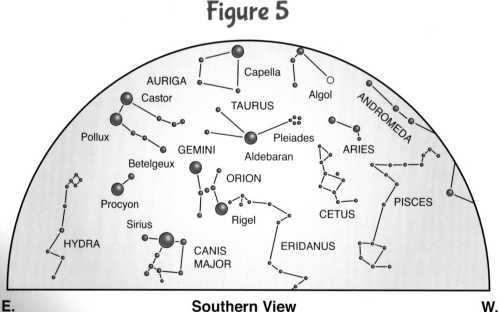

AURIGA
Capella
Castor
Algol
ANDROMEDA
TAURUS
Pollux
Pleiades
ARIES
GEMINI
Betelgeux
Aldebaran
ORION
Procyon
PISCES
Sirius
Rigel
CETUS
HYDRA
CANIS
MAJOR
ERIDANUS

E.   **Southern View**   **W.**

Sirius is the bright star in the constellation Canis Major (Big Dog). It is southeast of the constellation Orion (the Hunter). Both are easily seen in the winter and early spring skies.

2. Look for these constellations. Can you find Orion's belt? Do you see the "dog" in Canis Major?

Orion lights up the winter sky.

The Hour: A Logical Unit of Time

A number of early cultures divided daylight into twelve parts, which they called hours. We still use hours to mark the time with watches and clocks. Ancient cultures, however, used a stick's shadow. The shadow of a stick was the world's first "hour hand." Let's make a shadow clock and discover how it works.

Experiment 8: A Shadow Clock

Things You Will Need:

- tape
- sheet of paper
- square board or sheet of cardboard
- sunny place that is level
- stones
- clay
- pencil or stick
- clock or watch
- pen or pencil
- calendar

1. Tape a sheet of paper to a square board or sheet of cardboard. Shortly after sunrise, place the board in a sunny place that is level. Several stones can be added to keep the board in place.

2. Use a piece of clay to support an upright pencil or stick near the middle of the south end of the board. (See Figure 6.) The pencil or stick is called a gnomon.

Figure 6

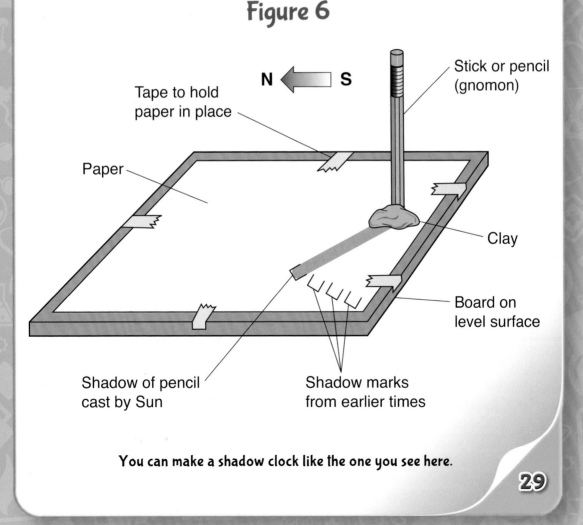

N ⬅ S

Stick or pencil (gnomon)

Tape to hold paper in place

Paper

Clay

Board on level surface

Shadow of pencil cast by Sun

Shadow marks from earlier times

You can make a shadow clock like the one you see here.

3. Use a second pencil to mark the end of the stick's shadow and the time. Do this about every hour until sunset. What happens to the length of the shadow as the day progresses? What happens to the direction of the shadow as the day progresses?

4. Is your shadow clock still accurate the next day? A week later? A month later?

Experiment 9: Making a Sundial

Things You Will Need:

- an adult
- North-south line from Experiment 2
- Internet access, map, or globe
- board about 30 cm (1 ft) on each side
- board about 1.25 cm (0.5 in) thick
- glue

- 2 wooden blocks
- time of midday (from a local paper or the Internet)
- sunny day
- clock
- marking pen
- protractor
- ruler

It's best to build a sundial in the summer when there are more hours of sunlight.

1. Find the latitude where you live by looking on the Internet. A reasonable estimate can be made using a map or globe. Your sundial's gnomon (the upright piece that casts a shadow) will be cut at an angle equal to your latitude.

2. A board about 30 cm (1 ft) on each side can be the base of your sundial (Figure 7).

3. The gnomon can be made from a board about 1.25 cm (0.5 in) thick. The gnomon should have a triangular shape. The angle at its south end should be cut at an angle equal to your latitude. (**Ask an adult to cut the board.**)

4. Glue the gnomon to the board. Support it with blocks so it stays upright until the glue dries.

5. Find the time of midday in a local paper or on the Internet.

6. Begin the experiment on a sunny day a few minutes before midday. Place the sundial near or on the north-south line you made in Experiment 2.

7. At precisely midday, the gnomon's shadow will point due north. A line through the center of that shadow can be labeled "12." There will be no shadow on either side of the gnomon.

Figure 7

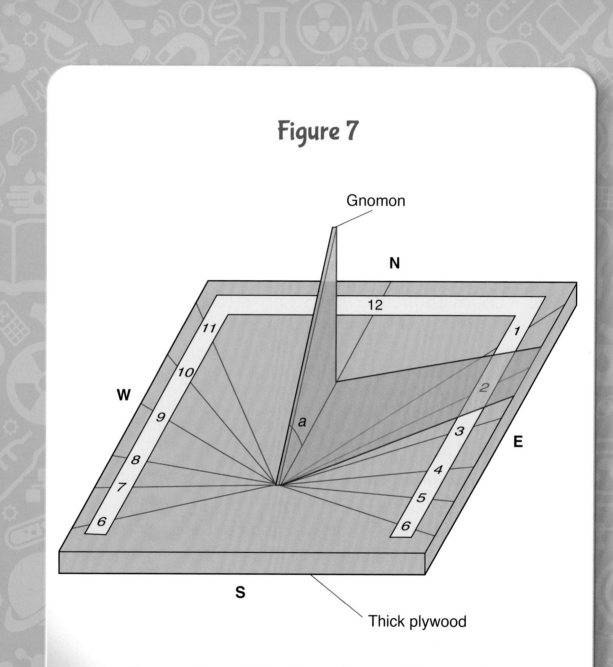

Gnomon

N

12

11

1

10

W

2

9

a

3

E

8

4

7

5

6

6

S

Thick plywood

You can make a sundial like this one from wood. Be sure angle a, the angle at the gnomon's base, equals your latitude. What time is it according to this sundial?

8. Exactly one hour later, draw a line along the outer edge of the shadow cast by the gnomon. It should be marked 1.

9. Continue to mark lines using the gnomon's shadow every hour until sunset.

10. For the morning hours, draw the mirror image of the afternoon lines on the other side of the gnomon. For example, measure the angle between the gnomon and the 1:00 p.m. line. Draw a line at the same angle on the other side of the gnomon and label it 11. The 10:00 a.m. line will make the same angle as the 2:00 p.m. line, and so on. You now have a "clock" that will measure sun time. It will seldom agree with clock time.

The Hour: An Explanation

A shadow clock is not very accurate. After a few days, the time of sunrise changes. The shadow clock will no longer be accurate according to a clock. Of course, ancient cultures were not as concerned about accurately marking time.

A sundial is more accurate because the gnomon is cut at the angle of your latitude. But it too loses accuracy as the time of midday changes.

Time Around the Earth

Earth is very nearly a sphere (it bulges a bit at the equator). Earth's equator and lines of latitude circle the globe. (If you have a globe, it would help to have one on hand. You can also refer to the videos in the Learn More section for more on longitude and latitude.) There are 360 degrees in a circle. We divide a day into 24 hours. Dividing 360 degrees by 24 hours gives us 15 degrees per hour. So the sun appears to move around Earth at a speed of 15 degrees per hour. Of course, it is Earth that turns eastward at 15 degrees per hour.

So that all countries can agree on time, Earth is divided into 24 time zones. This division is based roughly on lines of longitude. (See Figure 8.) A line of longitude passing through Greenwich, England, is the prime meridian. It is the meridian chosen to be zero degrees longitude.

Moving west from Greenwich, the zones decrease from 0 to −12 at approximately 15-degree intervals. Moving east from Greenwich, the zones increase from 0 to +12 at approximately 15-degree intervals.

The time east of Greenwich increases by one hour every 15 degrees. The time west of Greenwich decreases by one hour about every 15 degrees. (See Figure 8.) If it is noon in Greenwich, it is 7:00 a.m., five hours earlier,

Figure 8

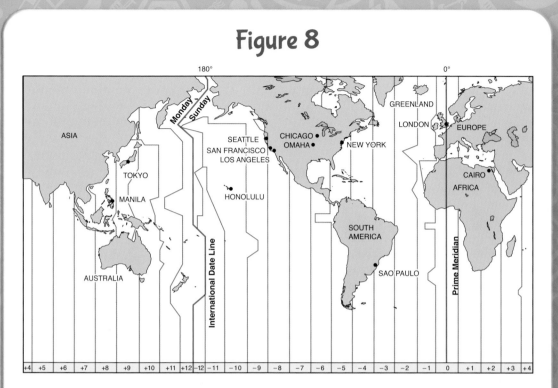

Earth is divided into twenty—four time zones. Each zone is about fifteen degrees wide. At the equator the zones are about 1,670 kilometers (1,000 miles) wide. At the poles, their widths are zero. The prime meridian (0° longitude) goes through Greenwich, England. The International Dateline is a north—south line across the Pacific Ocean.

in New York. In Tokyo, it is 9:00 p.m., nine hours later. Remember, Earth turns from west to east.

Running north-south across the middle of the Pacific Ocean is the International Date Line. When you cross that line going west, you add one day. If you are traveling east, you subtract one day. If it's 6:00 a.m. on Tuesday, July 10 east of the date line, it's 6:00 a.m. on Wednesday, July 11, west of the date line.

The Royal Observatory in Greenwich, England, is at 0 degrees longitude.

Experiment 10: Crossing the International Date Line

To see that the International Date Line makes sense, try this experiment.

Things You Will Need:

⦿ Figure 8

1. Start at New York City. Assume it's 1:00 p.m. on a Tuesday.
2. Move west, making a quick around-the-world "map trip."
3. Don't forget to add a day when you cross the International Date Line.
4. Remember, a new day starts at midnight.

    What day and time is it when you get back to New York City?

Time Zones and Railroads

In the United States, before 1883, each community set its clocks according to sun time. Noon was at midday. When it was noon in Albany, New York, cities west of Albany were at an earlier time. It was about 11:40 a.m.

in Buffalo, New York, and about 11:50 a.m. in Syracuse, New York.

By the late nineteenth century, people commonly traveled by train. But preparing a time schedule for arrivals and departures was difficult. Moving east or west, the clock at every station showed a different time.

In October, 1883, railroad companies agreed to divide the continental United States into four time zones (see Figure 9). Albany, Buffalo, and Syracuse, were in the Eastern Time Zone. All three cities would now have the same time. Clocks in Chicago, and all clocks in the Central Time Zone, would be an hour earlier. San Francisco, and all clocks in the Pacific Time Zone, would be three hours earlier. So railroad travel over one hundred years ago helped determine the current time displayed on your clock!

Figure 9

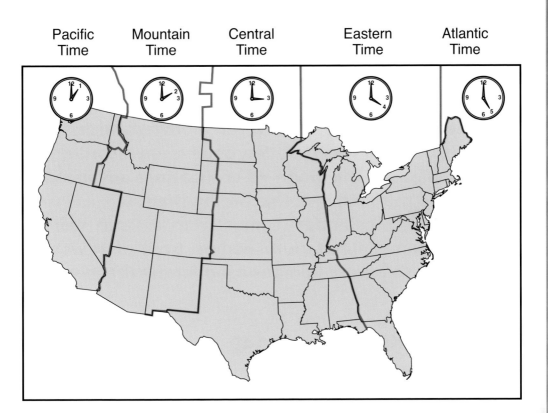

Pacific Time · Mountain Time · Central Time · Eastern Time · Atlantic Time

Railroad companies introduced time zones across the continental United States in 1883. The zones allowed railroad companies to easily make timetables for arrivals and departures.

Calendars: A Human Invention

While we've thus far explored mostly natural units of time, time zones are an example of how humans have influenced the way time is measured and recorded. Another human invention is the calendar. Archaeologists have discovered notched sticks at least 30,000 years old that they believe are recordings of the phases of the moon. As civilizations advanced, so too did their means of recording time.

The word "calendar" comes from a Latin word *calendarium*. *Calendarium* comes from the word *calendae*. It's a word Romans used for the first day of each month.

The Early Roman Calendar

The earliest Roman calendar had only ten months: Martius (March), Aprilis, (April), Maius (May), Iunius (June), Quintilis (July), Sextilis (August), September, October, November, and December. In Latin, *octo* means eight. An octagon has eight sides and October was the eight month of the year. What other months indicated their numerical position in the year?

A Problem to Solve: The Early Roman Calendar

The names and the number of days in each month in the Roman calendar are shown in Table 1. The table also gives their present names and lengths.

How many days were there in the Roman year?

How do you think they managed the missing days? During what season did these missing days occur?

Table 1:
The Roman Calendar

Name of month	Length in Days	Present Name	Length in Days
Martius	31	March	31
Aprilis	30	April	30
Maius	31	May	31
Iunius	30	June	30
Quintilis	31	July	31
Sextilis	30	August	31
September	30	September	30
October	31	October	31
November	30	November	30
December	30	December	31

Around 700 BCE, King Numa Pompilius added the months of Januarius (30 days) and Februarius (29 days) to precede Martius. However, this new calendar was still 2.25 days short of a year.

The Julian Calendar

By 46 BCE, the seasons were no longer in agreement with the calendar. Julius Caesar took action. He hired Sosigenes, an astronomer, to fix the calendar for the entire Roman Empire. Sosigenes established what was basically our present calendar. He knew it took 365.25 days for the sun to return to its exact position in the sky. To take account of the extra six hours (1/4 day), he invented the leap year.

To move the spring equinox back to March, Caesar added, by decree, 80 days to the year we call 46 BCE. To those living at that time, it was known as the "year of confusion." Caesar put his revised calendar into effect on January 1, 45 BCE.

Romans believed uneven numbers were lucky. So the odd-numbered months (Januarius, Martius, Maius, Quintilis, September, and November) were 31 days long. After Julius Caesar died, Quintilis was renamed July to honor him. Later, Sextilis was renamed August to honor Augustus Caesar who succeeded Julius as emperor. August was then assigned 31 days to improve its luck at the cost of February, which was reduced to 28 days, except on leap years when it had 29.

The Gregorian Calendar

The Julian calendar worked well for many years. However, a year is 11 minutes and 14 seconds less than 365.25 days. By 1582, that small time difference was causing a problem. The vernal equinox (when the sun reaches the equator and spring begins) was occurring in early March rather than around March 21.

To Christians, the vernal equinox is very important. It has a role in determining the date of Easter. Easter is the time when Jesus was believed to have been resurrected. Easter's date was established at the Council of Nicaea in 325 CE. It is the first Sunday following the first full moon after the vernal equinox. To move the vernal equinox back to late March, Pope Gregory XIII made two changes to the Julian calendar. First, he decreed that the day following October 4, 1582, would be October 15. This moved all following dates, including the vernal equinox, forward ten calendar days.

Second, he changed leap year to make the average calendar year closer to 365.25 days minus 11 minutes and 14 seconds, or 365.2422 days. The leap year would continue as always except when it came to centuries. It would only occur on centuries divisible by 4. As a result, 1700, 1800, and 1900 were not leap years but 1600 and 2000 were.

With these changes in place, the Gregorian calendar will be off by only one day in 3,300 years—plenty of time to fix the calendar again.

Catholic countries, such as Italy and Spain, adopted the Gregorian calendar in October 1582. Protestant countries, such as Great Britain and her American colonies, delayed acceptance for many years. The difference in dates are often indicated by the words "old style" to show that the date is based on the Julian calendar. The photo on the next page shows the use of old style in dating the first encounter between the pilgrims and Native Americans on Cape Cod, Massachusetts.

In 1752, Great Britain and its colonies converted to the Gregorian calendar. Twelve days were lost when Parliament ruled that September 2, 1752, would be followed by September 14. Many other countries did not change to the Gregorian calendar for another century or more.

One Mile West of this site
Hostile Indians had their

FIRST ENCOUNTER

6 December 1620
(OLD STYLE)

WITH MYLES STANDISH, JOHN CARVER,
WILLIAM BRADFORD, EDWARD WINSLOW,
JOHN TILLEY, EDWARD TILLEY, JOHN
HOWLAND, RICHARD WARREN, STEPHEN
HOPKINS, EDWARD DOTEY, JOHN ALLERTON,
THOMAS ENGLISH, MASTER MATE CLARK,
MASTER GUNNER COPIN AND THREE
SAILORS OF THE MAYFLOWER COMPANY

THIS TABLET IS PLACED IN 1920 BY THE
SOCIETY OF COLONIAL WARS IN THE
COMMONWEALTH OF MASSACHUSETTS

Notice the use of "old style" on this tablet. It appears under the date, which was 6 DECEMBER 1620. This tablet is near the site of the first hostile encounter between pilgrims and Native Americans on Cape Cod, Massachusetts. What was the date according to the Gregorian calendar?

In this book you've seen how both nature and man helped shape the way in which we tell and record time. Hopefully you have a better appreciation for something we usually take for granted. You can learn more about the world around you by taking a look at the other books in this series, which investigate color, light, sound, stars, and animals. Keep exploring, scientist!

GLOSSARY

analemma—A plot resembling a figure 8 that shows the difference between sun time and clock time.

ellipse—A shape that looks like a squashed circle. Earth's orbit around the sun is elliptical.

full moon—The phase of the moon when it is fully illuminated and on the opposite side of Earth from the sun.

latitude—An imaginary line around Earth that runs east to west and is parallel to the equator.

longitude—An imaginary circle that passes through the north and south poles at right angles to the equator.

mean solar day—The average length of a solar day. Using the mean solar day eliminates the need to constantly change our clocks.

meridian—A circle that runs north-south passing through the poles and a particular place. The prime meridian (0 degrees) passes through Greenwich, England.

midday—The point during a day at which the sun is halfway across the sky (rarely at noon).

new moon—The time during which the moon is between Earth and the sun.

sidereal day—The time it takes Earth to complete one rotation relative to a particular star. It is about four minutes shorter than a mean solar day.

solar day—The time between successive passings of the sun over the same meridian (line of longitude).

LEARN MORE

Books

Formichelli, Linda. *Timekeeping: Explore the History and Science of Telling Time With 15 Projects.* White River Junction, VT: Nomad Press, 2012.

Jenkins, Martha. *The Time Book: A Brief History From Lunar Calendars to Atomic Clocks.* London: Walker Books Ltd., 2010.

Pohlen, Jerome. *Albert Einstein and Relativity for Kids: His Life and Ideas With 21 Activities and Thought Experiments.* Chicago: Chicago Review Press, 2012.

Websites

Easy Science for Kids
easyscienceforkids.com/all-about-ancient-and-modern-calendars/
Some interesting facts about time and calendars and a fun short video.

NeoK12
neok12.com/Time.htm
Videos designed for older kids that might be fun to watch with an adult.

Science Kids
sciencekids.co.nz/sciencefacts/time.html
A quick link to some time facts.

Social Studies for Kids
socialstudiesforkids.com/subjects/timeinhistory.htm
A site examining how time has been measured throughout history.

INDEX